BOOK ANALYSIS

Written by Ludivine Auneau and
Paola Livinal
Translated by Rebecca Neal

Mend the Living

by Maylis de Kerangal

MAYLIS DE KERANGAL

FRENCH WRITER

- **Born in Toulon in 1967.**
- **Notable works:**
  - *Birth of a Bridge* (2010, first English translation published 2014), novel
  - *Mend the Living* (2014, first English translation published 2016), novel

Maylis de Kerangal initially worked for the French publishing company Éditions Gallimard, before founding her own publishing house focused on children's literature, Le Baron Perché. She now works full-time as a writer and has published over 15 books to date, all of which received significant media attention upon their release in her native France. Her first novel, *Corniche Kennedy*, was published in 2008 to popular and critical acclaim, and she won the Prix Médicis for *Birth of a Bridge* in 2010 and the Prix Landerneau for *Tangentes vers l'est* in 2012. Her greatest success, however, came in 2014, when her captivating novel *Mend the Living* (also published in English as

The Heart: A Novel) won multiple literary awards.

MEND THE LIVING

A HEART'S JOURNEY

- **Genre:** novel
- **Reference edition:** De Kerangal, M. (2016) *Mend the Living*. Trans. Moore, J. London: MacLehose Press.
- **1st edition:** 2014
- **Themes:** bereavement, organ donation, heart, transplant, life, death

Mend the Living follows a heart during the process of a transplant over a period of 24 hours. It is a polyphonic novel, featuring the voices of the loved ones of Simon (a young man who has been left braindead after a car accident and whose heart is about to be transplanted into someone else), the doctors, nurses and surgeons who treat him, and the patient who receives his heart. Interestingly, Simon's voice is the only one that is not heard. The organ donation has a major impact on all the characters: it inspires panic, pain, reflection and hope in equal measure, and marks an ending for some but a new beginning for others. The novel won a number of literary prizes, including the Prix Orange du Livre 2014 and the Grand prix RTL-Lire 2014 in France, and the Wellcome Prize 2017 in Britain.

SUMMARY

The importance of life is at the heart of *Mend the Living*, as is clearly illustrated in its title. The novel opens with three young surfers admiring the terrible beauty of the waves and feeling heroic as they do battle with the sea. However, the real drama comes later: when Simon is killed in a car accident, his parents have to decide whether or not to donate his organs, which could save the lives of total strangers. By considering Simon's sudden death in this light, his family are able to overcome their pain and go on living. However, first of all there is a race against the clock to remove, transport and transplant his organs while they are still viable.

Simon and his friends Chris and John devote every weekend to their shared passion, surfing. When he gets up on that fateful Sunday, the 19-year-old has no idea that that day will be the last time he will ever ride the waves and kiss his beautiful girlfriend Juliette, or that his heart will soon beat in the chest of Claire Méjan, a woman in her early fifties suffering from an inflammation of her cardiac muscles. On the way back from the beach, Chris falls asleep at the wheel and loses control of his car. Simon, who is sitting in the middle without a seatbelt, is thrown forwards into the windscreen.

By the time he gets to the hospital, it is too late: the damage to his brain is too severe, and after several examinations, Dr Pierre Revol and one of his colleagues declare him braindead.

Simon's mother Marianne has been told about the accident, but she does not yet know how serious it was. She is thrown into a state of panic and tries in vain to contact Simon's father Sean, from whom she has been separated for years. She quickly drops off her 7-year-old daughter Lou at a neighbour's house and rushes to be with her son. Left to face the situation alone, she gets more and more worried the closer she gets to the hospital.

When she sees the way the medical staff (including the nurse Cordelia Owl) behave around her, Marianne quickly realises that her son's condition is serious. Dr Revol tells her that Simon is in a coma and that the situation is irreversible, but he does not feel that it is time to broach the subject of his death yet. This means that the two of them end up talking at cross-purposes: when the doctor asks her about Simon's general health, Marianne thinks that he is preparing for her son's recovery, but Revol knows how things are going to turn out and actually has organ donation in mind.

The surgeon immediately contacts Thomas Remige, a nurse who helps to coordinate organ removals: where his work ends, his colleague's begins. Remige has the unenviable task of breaking the news of Simon's death to his parents and asking them if they will consent to organ donation. He knows that it is a delicate subject and reactions can vary greatly depending on the family in question, but nonetheless he has to bring it up as soon as possible, because in these situations, time is of the essence.

Meanwhile, Marianne agrees to meet Sean in a bar, a neutral space which does not stir up bad memories for either of them. She had previously pictured their meeting very differently: there was a time when she thought she would make herself beautiful and attractive to the man she once loved. Instead, she is dishevelled, grief-stricken and almost unrecognisable. As soon as Sean sees his ex-wife, he throws himself into her arms and they share an embrace, united in their fear for their son. She tells him what Dr Revol said to her, and when he hears the word "irreversible", its terrifying finality gives him a burning urge to lash out and destroy everything.

When they return to the hospital, the announcement that Simon is dead leaves them shellshocked and cruelly snatches away their last shred of hope. The news is all the more difficult to take because his heart is still beating and his warm, rosy skin makes it look as though he is just sleeping. His parents struggle to understand what is happening, and Sean asks why he is being kept alive artificially if there is no hope of recovery. This is Remige's cue to bring up the possibility of organ donation.

The conversation goes badly: Simon's parents cannot contemplate donating their son's organs while they are still struggling to come to terms with his death. Sean flies off the handle, talks about his son as if he were still alive, and refuses point-blank to consider the donation. As the parents seem to be a lost cause, Remige leaves them alone to grieve and think things over. Marianne manages to calm Sean down and talk him round by getting him to understand that Simon will not suffer.

From that point on, the pace picks up, as the medical staff have to consider not only the donor, but the many potential recipients whose lives would be changed forever by a new heart. This calls for the help of Marthe Carrare, a doctor at the Agency of Biomedicine tasked with using a range of criteria to determine who will receive the organ and with keeping the donor and the potential recipients anonymous. By now, the only thing connecting Simon Limbeau to his liver, lungs, kidneys and heart is an ID number.

The doctor calls the various hospitals which could receive the organs. This is a very quick process, as the hospitals only have 20 minutes to accept the donation. There is a representative of each hospital in the operating room, tasked with removing the organ, transporting it and transplanting it into the patient immediately. The surgeon Virgilio Breva removes Simon's heart and takes it to the Pitié-Salpêtrière hospital in Paris.

While Marianne and Sean are reflecting on their decision and wondering whether Simon's memories and his love for Juliette will go with his heart, Claire Méjan is worrying about the prospect of living with a heart that is not her own. She struggles with the painful knowledge that, in order for her to live, someone else must die. While Claire informs her family and prepares to go into hospital, Simon's parents must face up to reality and tell their loved ones that their son has died.

Simon's fight is over, but he dies a hero, giving his body to help others. His lifeless body in the operating theatre is a distressing sight, and it is now time to sew up the incisions and hand him back to his parents. Thomas Remige, who has stayed with him, sings to him in a scene reminiscent of a funeral rite.

As Simon leaves the world, a part of him lives on. At 5:49 in the morning, Claire Méjan feels a new heart beating within her.

CHARACTER STUDY

SIMON LIMBEAU

Simon Limbeau is 19 years old, and spends his free time on the beaches of Le Havre with his friends. He is a dreamer, loves his girlfriend and lives life to the full until it is snatched away from him.

Although he is the novel's main character, we know very little about him, because his heart plays a more important role in the plot than his personality. The other characters, and the reader, try to imagine what he would have wanted: "for example, we might ask whether Simon was a believer, or whether he was generous". Another key issue is whether he was for or against organ donation. This raises an existential question: is a person more than the sum of their physical parts? Will the heart that has been cut out of the teenage boy's chest still carry all his feelings and memories? Indeed, Simon's parents wonder what will become of his love for Juliette once his heart beats in someone else's body.

After the operation to remove Simon's vital organs, the doctors even implicitly compare him to a Greek hero: "funerary rituals come to mind, ones that conserve the beauty of the Greek hero come to die with intention on the battlefield […]".

MARIANNE LIMBEAU

Marianne Limbeau is Simon and Lou's mother. She has been separated from their father, Sean, for several years, and is the first person to find out about her son's accident.

Throughout the novel, the former couple put aside their differences to support one another. Although they do not talk much, they comfort each other through physical affection. On multiple occasions, Marianne has to calm Sean down.

The nurse in charge of coordinating organ donations sees her as "'the resource person': in other words, the one who could create a wake effect". His hunch proves correct, as she is the one who manages to persuade her ex-husband to agree to the organ donation. Marianne and Sean's shared pain brings them together, and they are seized by a desire to rebuild their family. They act like a couple, causing Lou to ask in surprise whether they are back together. They hope that, together, the three of them can find the strength to move past this tragic event.

SEAN

Sean shares his son's taste for adventure. After a spell canoeing around New Zealand, he now makes his living building surfboards, kayaks and other small boats.

After he finds out the devastating news, he loses his temper more than once. When he is in the bar with Marianne, he is propelled out of his seat by the desire to break something, and he lashes out at Thomas Remige when he brings up organ donation, telling him: "Simon's body is not a warehouse of organs you can just lay your hands on". Marianne's gentle touch manages to soothe him, and she is the one who has the strength to make the important decisions and break the news of Simon's death to their loved ones. When he is at his lowest ebb, his ex-wife supports and comforts him.

PIERRE REVOL

Pierre Revol is a doctor in the intensive care unit. He is described as "a tall man, skinny, thorax hollowed and belly round – solitude – long arms long legs, white leather lace-ups, something slender and uncertain in him that matches his juvenile mien". He is the first person to see Simon at the hospital and assess his condition. He is also the person who has to talk to the family and tell them that Simon is in a coma and his condition is irreversible. He weighs his words carefully and takes measured pauses to allow Marianne to come to terms with the terrible news.

There is a reason he chose to work in the ICU: in this department, which "houses these bodies situated exactly at the points between life and death", he constantly experiences "the stark consciousness of his own existence". The clarity his work brings him allows him to face death and the bereaved families, and to identify the dead and set the organ donation process in motion (or not, as the case may be).

THOMAS REMIGE

After extensive training, Thomas Remige is "one of the three hundred organ donation specialists in the country". Still aged just 29, he is renowned for the quality of his work. He is gentle yet firm in his conversations with families, as he knows that the issue of organ donation is a delicate one and that no two families react to it in exactly the same way. This means that he has to adapt his approach and try to find the right moment to broach the subject.

In Simon's case, his father forces Remige to bring the subject up by asking why his son is hooked up to artificial breathing apparatus if his condition is irreversible: "[Sean's question] interrupts the protocol's timeline [...]. It's a cry he must answer. He decides to speak to them now". He asks Simon's parents to think about what he would have wanted and what his personality was like, but he does not put any pressure on them: "Thomas has adopted the principle of absolute respect of the family's decision, and also understands this indisputable aspect – the body of the deceased is sacred for his loved ones".

His role is to obey the wishes of the deceased's loved ones. This is why he plays the sound of the waves to Simon just before his heart is removed and "whispers that Sean and Marianne are with him, and Lou, too, and Grammy; he murmurs that Juliette is there", "even though he knows that his words sink into a lethal void". He enjoys singing, and uses it as a way of soothing Simon's body and demonstrating his respect, almost like a religious ceremony, so that he may rest in peace.

MARTHE CARRARE

"Marthe Carrare is a short woman, around sixty, olive-skinned", and works as a doctor at the Agency of Biomedicine. Her job is to ensure that the donors remain anonymous and that the organs can be traced. She is the connection between Simon and the potential recipients; it is up to her to identify the best candidates, make the case for the transplant in the various hospitals and deal with logistics so that the organ reaches the patient in time. She does not know Simon and never sets eyes on him: she is just one link in the complex chain of organ donation.

VIRGILIO BREVA

Personal interest in heart surgery

The team at the Pitié-Salpêtrière hospital in Paris comprises the surgeon Virgilio Breva and his intern Alice. However, above them both is Harfang, a big name at the hospital who comes from a long line of doctors. He is the man to impress by demonstrating skill under pressure, and this is what Virgilio is working towards. Virgilio is insecure about his appearance and hopes to emulate Harfang by becoming a renowned doctor and seducing beautiful women.

He is an expert heart surgeon, and enjoys handling the organ and performing transplants. His branch of medicine involves cutting open, stitching together, mending and restarting ailing bodies.

Lack of interest in patients

His behaviour towards Simon is detached, and he shares the same concerns as most people. When he finds out that he has a surgery to perform that evening, his mind immediately jumps to the

France vs. Italy football match that he will miss that night and to his attractive girlfriend Rose. His task is to remove Simon's heart in Le Havre and transport it to Paris as quickly as possible in order to transplant it into his patient, Claire Méjan.

CLAIRE MÉJAN

Claire is 50 years old, but her heart is already failing: it is getting weaker all the time, and she could go into cardiac arrest at any moment. Since she needs a transplant as soon as possible, she has moved into a small apartment opposite the hospital in case she gets the call she is waiting for and needs to be there immediately. With her life hanging in the balance, she refuses to decorate her new home, because she knows it is only temporary.

She is not worried about the operation itself; rather, "What torments her is the idea of this new heart, that someone had to die today in order for all of this to happen, and that he or she could invade and transform her, change her". She feels even more guilty because "she will never be able to say thank you – and that's just it". She also has to mourn for her own heart, which has housed her feelings and emotions all her life, so that she can take on a new one with its own story. She wonders what the surgeons will do with her tired, damaged heart: "Maybe somewhere there's a junkyard for organs".

CORDELIA OWL

Cordelia Owl is a 25-year-old nurse who has just started work at the ICU. She treats Simon when he arrives at the hospital in the morning and is present when his organs are removed in the evening. At the hospital, she can be counted on to respond to any services, shortages or emergencies at a moment's notice.

However, she commits a breach of ethics as a result of a breakdown in communication, which is always a possibility in medical teams: she talks to Simon about the treatment she is going to carry out, because nobody has told her that he is already dead. The fact that a nurse is talking to their son makes it harder for his parents, who have just learnt of his death from Dr Revol, to come to terms with it. Cordelia then criticises Revol for his lack of teamwork and failure to communicate, as better communication can prevent misunderstandings and inconsistencies.

ANALYSIS

SIMILARITIES WITH THE EPIC

THE EPIC GENRE

An epic can be defined as "a long book, poem, or film, whose story extends over a long period of time or tells of great events" or "a long narrative poem recounting in elevated style the deeds of a legendary hero" (*Collins English Dictionary*).

Some of the most famous and enduring epics are the *Iliad* (8th century BCE) and the *Odyssey* (8th century BCE), both attributed to Homer (Greek poet, 8th century BCE), the *Aeneid* (29-19 BCE) by Virgil (Latin poet, 70-19 BCE) and *The Song of Roland* (late 11th century), a medieval French epic.

Although *Mend the Living* is not written in verse, it nonetheless resembles the epic in a number of ways.

Zero focalisation

In the Middle Ages, epics were recited with musical accompaniment in front of an audience by minstrels, who were both poets and musicians. During these performances, the minstrel would change into different costumes to play the various characters. The same thing occurs in this novel, as each chapter focuses on a different character so that the reader can see the story from multiple points of view. De Kerangal makes skilful use of zero focalisation (meaning that the narrator is omniscient and is privy to all the details of the story), giving us access to the entire story and to all the actions, thoughts and feelings of its various characters.

The focus on a hero

At the heart of the plot is a hero who is unusual because he is unconscious. Simon was surfing that very morning, but by the evening he is sacrificing his body for others (quite literally, as he is donating his organs). Because of this, he is repeatedly described in heroic terms, calling to mind ancient heroes who voluntarily sacrificed themselves for the greater good.

Simon is also depicted as a Christ-like figure, thus echoing the supernatural Christian dimension of certain medieval and modern epics. When his organs are removed, he is described in a way that is reminiscent of Jesus on the cross, and the incisions on his abdomen recall the wounds in Christ's side.

Remige is linked to goldfinches in the story: he expresses a desire to listen to or to own one, and his surname means "feather" or "quill" in French. This implicitly connects him with Simon, as the goldfinch is present in some depictions of the Virgin and child (see, for example, *Madonna of the Goldfinch* [1506] by Raphael [Italian painter and architect, 1483-1520]). The goldfinch in this painting also foreshadows Christ's sacrifice: its red forehead symbolises the blood spilt during his crucifixion, while the thistle it feeds on brings to mind the crown of thorns.

An account of great deeds

The actions carried out by the medical staff during the organ transplant can also be compared to the great deeds accomplished by a person or group that form the basis of epics.

Medical advances, along with developments in transport and IT, allow organs to be transplanted safely. This technological progress is complemented by a human dimension, comprised of such qualities as skill, passion, challenge and ambition (as displayed by Virgilio Breva). All these elements, both technical and human, are needed to carry out the operation successfully.

Given the energy and skill that the transplant requires and the number of things that could go wrong, it would not be an exaggeration to describe it as a great deed. The removal of the organs in particular is described as though it were an extraordinary feat on the battlefield: the entire scene is permeated with words associated with war and death, such as "chaos", "blood", "battlefield", "violence" and "blade".

Finally, Thomas Remige's voice predominates in this scene. Like in epic poems, singing is central to this part of the story, because it raises Simon above ordinary mortals, soothes him and rights the wrongs inflicted on his body.

DEATH IN A NEW LIGHT

During an international conference on neurology at the Claude-Bernard hospital in Paris in 1959, Maurice Goulon (French professor of medicine, 1919-2008) and Pierre Mollaret (French neurologist and biologist, 1898-1987) put forward the claim that humans do not die when their heart stops beating, but when their brain ceases to function. In other words, "I don't think anymore, therefore I am no more". This new definition of death "could also pave the way for organ recovery and transplantation".

However, this is not how we tend to imagine a dead body: a person who is braindead still has a heartbeat, rosy skin and a warm body. This makes it difficult for Marianne and Sean to come to terms with their son's death, because they are unable to connect the internal damage he has sustained with his peaceful exterior.

The media also influences our conception of death, as it does not allow us to see it as it really is. Instead, many of us live in a world "where we're shielded from a view of death, where it's erased from the day-to-day, carried off to the hospital where it's handled by professionals", making it all the more difficult to move past the denial phase.

When Marianne and Sean see their braindead son, they still cling to a glimmer of hope, even though Revol tells them that Simon's condition is irreversible. They cannot help but think of all the stories they have heard or read about patients who woke up after years in a coma, doctors who made mistakes and files that were accidentally switched.

Marianne and Sean have to start thinking about what comes next before they have even had time to come to terms with their son's death. Remige observes that "They're speaking of their son in the present, this is not a good sign", and consequently thinks that they will refuse to consent to the transplant. Before long, "They're speaking in the past [...]. For Thomas, this is a tangible step forward, the sign that the idea of their child's death is slowly crystallising". Even though they agree to organ donation, the reality of Simon's death does not sink in for his parents until his heart stops beating and his blood stops circulating. It is not until this point that Marianne feels a wave of calm wash over her and is sure that she has made the right choice.

THE SYMBOLIC SIGNIFICANCE OF THE HEART

The way we view the heart goes far beyond its organic function; we tend to see it as a symbol of love and the source of our feelings.

For example, Marianne describes Juliette as "Simon's heart" and wonders what will remain of his love for her after the transplant. Remige is well aware that "the symbolic charge differs from one organ to the next"; while Sean and Marianne are relatively happy to donate Simon's kidneys, lungs and liver, they are much more reluctant to let the surgeons remove his heart, as though this might take away a part of his soul. Claire, the recipient of Simon's heart, shares these fears, and is anxious at the prospect of seeing her own heart replaced by that of a stranger.

Furthermore, in the collective imagination, the heart represents life. In spite of Goulon and Mollaret's new definition of death, we still tend to think of the moment of death as the moment when the heart stops beating because it is the central organ in the body.

This is also one of the reasons that inspired Virgilio Breva to devote his life to heart surgery. He is a vain, insecure man who tries to defy destiny by gaining power over life and death, like a god: "Virgilio chose the heart in order to exist at the highest level, counting on the organ's sovereign aura to rain glory down upon him".

In the aftermath of her ordeal, Marianne throws herself into Sean and Lou's arms and feels their hearts beating: "if you come a little closer, if you are soft and silent, you can hear their hearts together, pumping the life that's left".

CHRONICLE OF A TRANSPLANT

Organ donation, the central theme of *Mend the Living*, is illustrated through the most symbolic of the organs with a heart transplant. De Kerangal describes the operation chronologically and in meticulous detail, and this accurate, well-researched account can be compared to a chronicle.

In reading the novel, French readers will learn that they too are potential organ donors, unless they have explicitly opted out or told their family that they do not want to donate (conversely, the UK uses an opt-in system, whereby individuals are not presumed to be organ donors unless they have signed up to the organ donor register). Most of this information is passed on to Sean and Marianne by Thomas Remige, who is in charge of coordinating organ and tissue donation. His tasks include supporting the family through the process, overseeing the restoration of the body after the organs have been removed, and returning the body to the family.

In the course of the transplantation process, the reader also learns about the workings of the Agency of Biomedicine, which is headquartered in Saint-Denis on the outskirts of Paris. Part of this organisation's role is to manage the database of people who have opted out of organ donation.

The character of Marthe Carrare serves to make the reader aware of all the work that goes into a successful transplantation, which is something of a race against time: in a very short period, suitable recipients have to be found, the relevant hospitals have to be contacted and logistics have to be coordinated.

The reader then witnesses the work of the team at the Pitié-Salpêtrière hospital after they receive their "treasure", which has arrived in time in spite of the delays that the vehicle transporting it encountered around Paris. The atmosphere is both peaceful and tense as they head to the operating room, where the transplant takes place immediately.

At the same time, we are given an insight into the life of Claire Méjan, who is going to receive Simon's heart, and all the preparations and worries that come with a heart transplant:

- almost a year ago, she moved to live as close to the hospital as possible in case a heart became available for her;
- her first transplant failed because her body rejected the new organ;
- she struggles with the idea that she it is waiting for someone else to die so that she can go on living;
- she regrets that she will never be able to thank the donor ("And above all, she will never be

able to say thank you").

Claire's preparation before she goes into the operating room is not described. After Simon's heart is transplanted into Claire's body, we are given an account of the restoration of his body, which spans an entire chapter and marks the end of this chronicle.

Thomas Remige oversees the restoration of the body, so that it can be handed back to the family in the same condition as before the surgery. Respect for the body during this process is vital, as in France failure to do so entails the risk of legal proceedings (*service-public.fr*).

The reader, who could one day be called on to donate their organs or make this decision for a loved one, will finish the novel with a much greater understanding of the heart transplant process.

THE IMPORTANCE OF TIME

The novel takes place over a period of 24 hours and is permeated by suspense, especially when the decision is made to remove the organs for transplantation, as each one can only survive outside the body for a set amount of time.

The beating of Simon's heart is described in the very first pages of the book. Initially, De Kerangal leads the reader to think that Simon will die while he is surfing with his friends, so there is a sense of mounting tension throughout this section of the story. In the end, nothing out of the ordinary happens, and the boys are described as though they are warriors or heroes: they call themselves "the *Big Wave Riders*" and enthuse "we're gonna be *kings!*". By the time they leave the beach, the tension has subsided and the reader is taken unawares by the crash which claims Simon's life.

How long will it take for Marianne and Sean to agree for their son's organs to be donated? They will only give their consent once they have accepted that their son is dead. It often takes longer for the dead person's loved ones to let go of their attachment to their body than it does for the organs to stop being viable. Thomas Remige has learnt to take a gentle approach to the painful process of securing the loved ones' consent as quickly as possible.

Once Simon's parents have given their consent, the next stage in the process quickly gets underway, because it also takes time to look for recipients. Fortunately, all the relevant files are now stored digitally. The organs have yet to be removed from the patient's body in Le Havre, and the recipient has to be chosen based on both medical and geographical criteria so that the transplant can be carried out in time. Once everything has been coordinated, it is now time for the process on the ground to get underway: "Coordinating teams have organised their transportation, called an airline that accepted this Sunday mission, and made sure that the little airport in Octeville-sur-Mer is open at night, formalising all the logistical details".

Time is also of the essence after the organ has been removed:

> "[...] and the crate they roll along the tarmac to the steps and hoist into the cabin, this matryoshka crate that holds the transparent plastic security bag that holds the container that holds the special jar that holds Simon Limbeau's heart – that holds nothing less than life itself – the potential for life, and that, five minutes later,

flies off into the air."

A combination of thoughtfulness, will, coordination and skill on the part of the various characters allows a heart in perfect condition to be removed from a young man and transplanted into a 50-year-old woman over 100 miles away in the space of just 24 hours.

While the characters are racing against time to keep Claire alive, Sean and Marianne are left devastated by Simon's death and feel deeply alone. Even as his organs are being removed, Marianne is unsure whether she has made the right decision. In the end, she looks into his face and finally feels a sense of calm.

FURTHER REFLECTION

SOME QUESTIONS TO THINK ABOUT...

- Why is Simon compared to a hero in the novel?
- Anaylse Thomas Remige's relationship with singing.
- Explain the meaning of the novel's title.
- How does the heart differ symbolically from the other organs?
- Comment on the following quotation: "[T]he heart exceeds the heart [...]. And even more, as the cutting-edge mechanic and ultrapowerful fantasy operator all rolled into one, Virgilio sees the heart as the linchpin of depictions (paintings, etc.) that organise the relation of the human being to the body, to other beings, to Creation, and to the gods".
- Why can it be difficult for recipients to accept an organ transplant? Use the novel to help you answer this question.
- Throughout history, humans have removed the organs, particularly the heart, from dead

bodies. Consider the example chosen by De Kerangal in the novel and compare it with older funerary rites or certain customs of war.

- In 1959, Maurice Goulon and Pierre Mollaret redefined death. Explain the changes this led to.
- Write a brief summary of an epic that is still well-known today and compare it to the operation carried out on Simon.
- In your opinion, why was this novel so successful?

We want to hear from you!
Leave a comment on your online library
and share your favourite books on social media!

FURTHER READING

REFERENCE EDITION

- De Kerangal, M. (2016) *Mend the Living*. Trans. Moore, J. London: MacLehose Press.

REFERENCE STUDIES

- Service-Public.fr (2016) *Prélèvement d'organes sur une personne décédée*. [Online]. [Accessed 5 January 2018]. Available from: <https://www.service-public.fr/particuliers/vosdroits/F183>

ADAPTATION

- *Heal the Living*. (2016) [Film]. Katell Quillévéré. Dir. France/Belgium: Les Flims du Bélier, Les Films Pelléas.

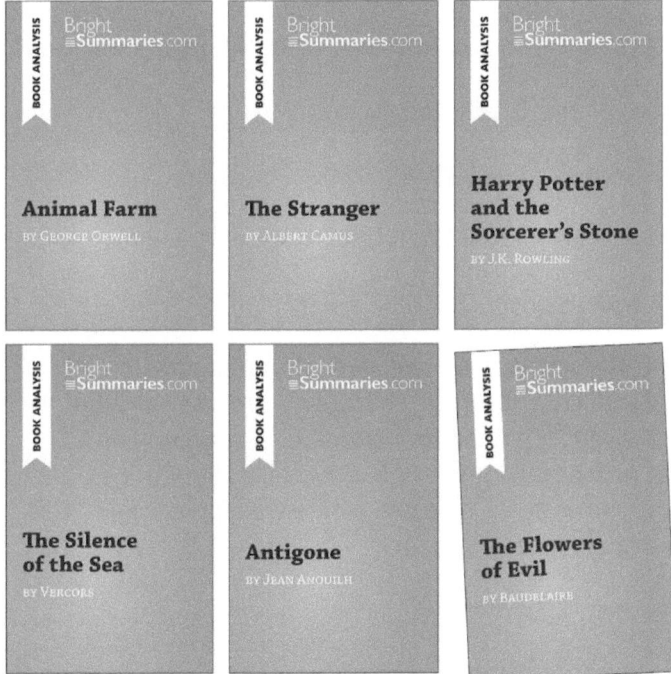

www.brightsummaries.com

Ebook EAN: 9782808007306

Paperback EAN: 9782808007849

Legal Deposit: D/2018/12603/2

This guide was written with the collaboration of Paola Livinal for the character studies of Virgilio Breva ("Personal interest in heart surgery") and Cordelia Owl, and for the sections "Similarities with the epic", "Chronicle of a transplant" and "The importance of time".

Cover: © Primento

Digital conception by Primento, the digital partner of publishers.